The Youth Worker's Handbook to

# FAMILY MINISTRY

# The Youth Worker's Handbook to
# FAMILY MINISTRY

### Strategies and practical ideas
### for reaching your students' families

by
## CHAP CLARK

**ZondervanPublishingHouse**

*Grand Rapids, Michigan*
*A Division of HarperCollinsPublishers*

*The Youth Worker's Handbook to Family Ministry: strategies and practical ideas for reaching your students' families*

©1997 by Youth Specialties, Inc.

Youth Specialties Books, 1224 Greenfield Dr., El Cajon, CA 92021, are published by Zondervan Publishing House, 5300 Patterson Ave. S.E., Grand Rapids, MI 49530.

---

**Library of Congress Cataloging-in-Publication Data**

Clark, Chap, 1954-
    The youth worker's handbook to family ministry : strategies and practical
ideas for reaching your students' families / Chap Clark.
      p.   cm.
    Includes index.
    ISBN 0-310-22025-4
    1. Church work with families.  2. Church group work with teenagers.  I. Title.
BV4438.C54   1997
259'.1—dc21                                        97-13808
                                                            CIP

---

*Edited by Randy Southern*
*Cover and interior design by Rogers Design & Associates*

*Printed in the United States of America*

97 98 99 00 01/ /5 4 3 2 1

# CONTENTS

**5** TAKING IT HOME
## Providing Materials to Strengthen Families Where They Live

### *Handouts for parents*

### *Handouts for teenagers*

# An Introduction to Family Ministry

Youth ministry in 1972 consisted of Sunday school classes, youth group meetings, rallies, concerts, special events, Bible studies, camps, and retreats. The excitement was obvious, the numbers were solid, and the kids were motivated to participate and grow in their faith.

Youth ministry at the same church 25 years later consists of Sunday school classes, youth group meetings, rallies, concerts, special events, Bible studies, camps, and retreats. The programming may be similar, but there are some stark differences between today's youth ministry and that of 1972. The most noticeable difference is the lack of spiritual depth, enthusiasm, and involvement on the part of today's students. *Boring* is the word of the day; self-focused faith reigns. Students graduate from a youth program they found irrelevant and unchallenging into an adult church "family" they have never really known or learned to care for. The result is church kids who have grown up without a love for the church, kids whose generation's hard-won independence from the establishment has cost them a meaningful connection to the body of Christ.

It was 25 years ago that youth ministers adopted the axiom, "Programs attract kids, relationships keep them," referring to relationships with adult sponsors. The reality today is that very little attracts kids. The handful of sponsors they see once or twice a week in front of a class or meeting cannot begin to meet the relational needs of today's kids. This generation of young people cannot be fooled and will not be won over by superficial relationships, marketed Christianity, or flashy programming. Relationships that are real, sustained, and even lifelong are what it takes to capture the hearts of today's young people. The culture has changed, and so must our approach to ministry.

## The Shift to Family Ministry

In the last few years a growing number of churches have begun a serious move toward something generically referred to as *family ministry.* Though still young, this movement is crossing boundaries of denomination, theology, and tradition.

Many churches want to get on board, but have little idea what family ministry is or what it really means for the church.

The confusion is understandable because family ministry looks different in almost every church. Some family ministries emphasize church-wide relationships, while others focus on programs and classes. Some care for hurting families and families in crisis, while others set their sights on drawing young people into the church family. Someday family ministry may have a consistent look, but for the next several years at least, every church's family ministry philosophy and program will differ at least slightly from everyone else's. Factors such as the church's history, needs, leadership, and perception account for these differences.

## The Purpose of The Youth Worker's Handbook to Family Ministry

This is a book for tired volunteer youth workers who know they need to become more family friendly, for seasoned professionals who are starting churches from scratch and want to do an entirely different kind of youth ministry, for family pastors who have no youth ministry experience or interest. In other words, this book is for anyone and everyone who wants to make a move toward a family ministry that works, regardless of theological, philosophical, or historical perspective. If you care at all about families—and especially for the church as family—this book is for you.

Remember that this book is a handbook—you can read it cover to cover if you want, but it is particularly intended to answer specific questions and issues as they arise.

Approach this book as you would family ministry—go as deep and as far as you like at a comfortable speed. Jump right in or gradually immerse yourself in the new and refreshing waters of caring for people as they are!

# DEFINING FAMILY MINISTRY

# 3 PERSPECTIVES OF FAMILY MINISTRY

Family ministry is not a new concept. It has been on the North American church agenda for decades. Unlike other areas of ministry focus, however, family ministry has emerged without any sort of across-the-board consensus of just what it is. Contemporary youth ministry in our culture, for example, has gone through an evolution of sorts, primarily driven by the successes of various parachurch movements over the last 60-plus years. Because of organizations like Young Life and Youth for Christ, youth ministries of all denominations and traditions have a great deal in common in terms of purpose, philosophy, and methodology.

Despite the recent explosion of church interest in family ministry, there has been no such widespread evolution of commonality among family ministry practitioners. The result has been a groundswell of individual organizations, authors, consultants, seminaries, and churches creating goals and plans in a near vacuum. Because of this lack of a common perception of family ministry, people responsible for family ministry in churches are often confused and frustrated as they set out to define for themselves and their church just what it is that they do.

There are currently three general working definitions of family ministry in our culture. Though they are still somewhat broad, these three different perspectives provide a starting point for anyone attempting either to develop a new family ministry or fine-tune an existing program.

## 1. The Therapeutic/Counseling Perspective

Probably the most widely used definition of family ministry, this perspective sees family ministry as primarily addressing the specific emotional and relational needs of a congregation. One family pastor described the programs in this type of ministry as providing both "guardrails" and "crisis medical centers" for people:

- The "guardrails" are preventive programs designed to strengthen family members (though the term *family* is rarely defined clearly) before they get in trouble. Programmatic examples include marriage seminars, parenting seminars, parent-youth communication courses, mutual understanding classes, and premarital counseling.

- The "crisis medical centers" are for those who have crashed through the "guardrails" and are in need of more specific help. Examples of these programs include divorce recovery workshops, marital and family counseling, and intervention programs. Generally the family ministers and pastors who lead these programs are licensed

Family ministry includes any services provided by a church or church agency, whether by a helping professional or by a nonprofessional volunteer, which aim to strengthen the relationships between family members.
—*Diana Garland and Diane Pancoast,* The Church's Ministry with Families

therapists and professional counselors who have a desire to serve in the church. (See "Family Ministry That Works" beginning on page 20 for more information on this perspective.)

### Strengths of the therapeutic/counseling perspective

This focus provides a necessary component to modern church ministry. Many people are hurting, bruised, and broken. The church must provide people, programs, and opportunities for healing and help as we build the body of Christ.

### Possible problems

Some people question whether the church's primary responsibility to families and individuals is to provide them with education and meetings. They suggest that people crave something more, something deeper from the church. An additional problem is that because this perspective is often limited to programs and education, the ministry events themselves are usually sparsely attended. Most people in the average pew are missed by these programs, as good as they may be.

## 2. The Nuclear Family Perspective

People who favor this perspective tend to believe that the basic function of family ministry is to equip and strengthen individual families in the church. Many practitioners of this model cite Old Testament passages to make a case for this focus.

Deuteronomy 4:9–10 and 11:18–21, for example, suggest that the primary training ground for discipleship and spiritual instruction is the nuclear family rather than the local church.

One pastor who prefers this perspective wanted to change the local church from a "church-based family ministry" to a "family-based church ministry." This subtle distinction lies in the nature of discipleship, training in the faith, and spiritual nurturing. The question is this: who is primarily responsible for these things—the church or the nuclear family (particularly the parents)?

Programs and philosophies that reflect the nuclear-family perspective include—

- Parent-training sessions

- At-home sex education

- A reduced emphasis on youth ministry as a separate entity

- An increased emphasis on parent-child programs such as retreats, service projects, and Sunday school classes

- A transfer of responsibility for the bulk of discipleship training from the church and to the home. (See "Family Ministry That Works" beginning on page 20 for more information on the nuclear-family perspective.)

Church family ministry needs to challenge Christians to expand the boundaries of the nuclear family, extending hospitality that enfolds others in expanded family systems.
—*David E. Garland,* A Biblical Foundation for Family Ministry

### Strengths of the nuclear family perspective

It is clear that throughout faith history God has desired the nuclear family to be the primary means of child discipleship. This ministry approach is designed to equip the family for its God-given assignment.

### Possible problems

Most parents feel inadequate to handle the task of leading their children closer to Jesus Christ in a meaningful way. Many parents feel guilty as it is when it comes to faith. Churches that place too great an emphasis on the responsibility of parents to disciple and nurture their kids can end up creating an even greater sense of parental frustration and guilt. If churches exert pressure on parents while offering little or no age-group-targeted ministry help (such as a vibrant youth ministry program), people may be lost. An additional problem is that the nuclear family perspective tends to ignore the needs and issues of "nontraditional" families who do not have the resources, health, or family system necessary to benefit from this emphasis.

## 3. The Church-as-a-Family Perspective

Those who work within this approach look at family ministry in a much broader sense than do supporters of the other perspectives. Relying primarily on the New Testament for support, those who hold to this view see the local church as God's model for the family. In Matthew 12:48-50, for

# The Brady Model...

example, Jesus asks, "Who is my mother, and who are my brothers?...For whoever does the will of my Father in heaven is my brother and sister and mother."

According to this model the church's primary function is to be such a close-knit faith community that individual nuclear families will be encouraged to draw together and not separate themselves. The "guardrails" and "crisis medical centers" of the therapeutic/counseling approach are also necessary in this model, but are usually part of a church's caring or counseling ministry instead of its family ministry.

Programs and philosophies that reflect this view include—

• An emphasis on intergenerational programs and activities (regardless of family composition or life stage).

• A congregational concern for and commitment to youth and children's ministries.

• A church-wide willingness to draw all programs into a single ministry focus of seeing themselves as part of a family and community. (See "Family

Ministry That Works" beginning on page 20 for more information on this perspective.)

## Strengths of the church-as-a-family perspective

This focus appears to best represent the New Testament expression of the local church. It does not dismiss or even diminish the role and responsibility of parents to raise their children in a household that serves the Lord; in fact, it strengthens and supports that role. For those who need extra help, due to family history, a relatively new or shallow faith, or any number of factors that would inhibit discipleship in the context of the nuclear family, the church provides an "extended family."

## Possible problems

When a church places a great deal of emphasis on community and fellowship, even above individual family needs and issues, it may ultimately hurt the individual family system. For example, a youth ministry program that has a strong small-group ministry and several high-powered weekly meetings may actually push a young person away from his family. After all, how can a night of playing board games and talking by a fire hope to compete with one hundred energetic kids cutting loose?

# FAMILY MINISTRY THAT WORKS

## The Wisdom of a Mix-and-Match Approach

There is not now, nor is there likely ever to be, an identifiable programmatic animal known as "family ministry." Every church and organization will have to decide three things as it attempts to create a workable family ministry:

**1.** What the people of the church and the surrounding community need,

**2.** How its own distinctiveness as an institution affects a family-friendly move, and

**3.** What resources—people, facilities, money, history—the church or organization has available to meet those needs.

It is important that, as churches and organizations evaluate their future, they do their best to cover all three models of family ministry: therapeutic/counseling, nuclear family, and church-as-a-family. (see the previous chapter for a discussion of these models). Effective family

> In short, family ministry is a total approach to families—an outlook. The essence of family ministry is an attitude toward the family that must be integrated into every aspect of church life. . . . The church is more like a family than anything else.
> —*Royce Money,*
> *Ministering to Families*

ministry is a three-pronged philosophy of how we "do church." It is not a program, but it will involve programs. It is not education, though it will offer some learning opportunities. It is rather a biblical way of caring for all persons, whatever their gender and age, whom we serve in the church of Jesus Christ.

## Three Components of Family Ministry That Works

### 1. Every church must have a counseling or care ministry.

A crucial and central role for the faith community since the beginning of time—from the Old Testament, through the ministry of Jesus and the apostles, and ever since—is to show mercy, tenderness, and compassion for the lost, broken, and bruised of the world. No matter what it is called, every church must have a care ministry that is equipped and committed to providing "guardrails" (preventative programs) and "medical centers" (caring, nurturing programs and people to help in times of crisis) for those both inside the church and in the dark, stale corners of every community. *

---

*Currently in more than 5,500 churches, Stephen Ministries are caring, supporting Christians who have a desire to be with one in a time of need, grief, or crisis. These trained lay members of the congregation visit one-on-one with hurting persons weekly, listen, offer resources and referrals (if needed), pray with and for them, and offer Christian love and support. For information about its complete system of training and organizing lay persons for caring ministry in and around their congregations, contact Stephen Ministries at (314) 645–5511 (8016 Dale, St. Louis, MO 63117–1449).

As necessary as it is, this care ministry should not be considered a church's only manifestation of family ministry. While a care ministry is vital to the health of the modern church, it will barely scratch the surface of the needs of the congregation, much less the community at large.

## 2. *Every church must take seriously the needs and issues of the nuclear family.*

**What family ministry is *not*:**
- Buildings or facilities
- Merely a catalogue of church or community programs
- Another appendage to a continually growing church program
- A passing fad
- Just for nuclear families— mom, dad, and children. It is relevant to everyone's needs.
- Just for church families
- Merely a counseling service
- Necessarily expensive

The nuclear family needs help. While youth workers and pastors fret about the lack of parental support for their youth ministry programs, the reality is that today's parents are lonelier, more fragmented, and more discouraged than ever before. As the culture races by at an incredible pace, the parents of today are running as fast as they can to simply keep up with their jobs, their money, their marriage, their schedules, and even their own health. Although they are being blamed for a lack of concern for their kids, many of today's parents are secretly crying, "Does anyone care about me?" The church must do all it can to care for and strengthen the fragile familial institution.

From ideas for parent training ("Workshops that Work," page 83) to a list of ways you can inadvertently damage a family ("If You Want to Hurt a Family, Do This," page 95), this book provides a truckload of practical information for making a difference in nuclear families. If churches and parachurch organizations make no other attempt at being family friendly, they must succeed at least here.

### 3. Every church must see itself as being the family of God—then program accordingly.

Jesus knew it and the writers of the New Testament knew it, but it seems the modern church has forgotten it: every person needs to be uniquely and intimately connected to other people in order to make sense of the life of faith. As hard as we try to individualize our religious experience, we cannot escape the fact that God created us to need each other. Jesus himself asked, "Who is my mother, and who are my brothers?" Pointing to his disciples, he said, "Here are my mother and my brothers. For whoever does the will of my Father in heaven is my brother and sister and mother" (Matthew 12:48–50).

The church is meant to be the people of God, a community of believers, and a family of faith—a central tenet in the Bible and in the history of the church.

# THE FRAGMENTED CHURCH

The modern church has been described as an octopus without a brain, a collection of arms acting independently with no central processing unit coordinating their actions. In many churches, especially large churches, when a specific ministry (youth ministry, for example) seems like an important next step, the solution is usually to simply start a program. Sometimes this process begins with the hiring of a staff person, but usually it involves the gathering of like-minded people to brainstorm ideas for the new project.

Soon there is a launch, the word goes out, and the program is off and running—a new entity in a sea of often disconnected entities, under the single umbrella of the local church. Before long this exciting, new, necessary, and cutting-edge vision becomes just one more program on the church bulletin, announcing to all that, indeed, the church can meet any need imaginable.

Ministries within the church typically end up competing for the space, money, resources, attention, focus, and time that programs need to flourish. Many modern churches have become a sanctified delicatessen—a delectable array of options from which to choose. Yet it's up to individuals to put together their own meals. This smorgasbord of programmatic competition ultimately creates a confused and divided congregation, as people wonder where to go to get involved in a meaningful way with God's people.

At its heart family-life ministry is related to the nature of the church, not merely to its work. Family-life ministry is not a mere appendage to the church's organization. Like missions, it must be integrated into the church's life.

—*Charles Sell,* Family Ministry

Structurally the worship service is viewed as one large entity; the other programs of the church are viewed as individual entities with their own worries, philosophies, passions, and champions. In most churches these programs are not linked practically or even philosophically to one another, and are, in fact, competitors. A diagram of this structure might something like this:

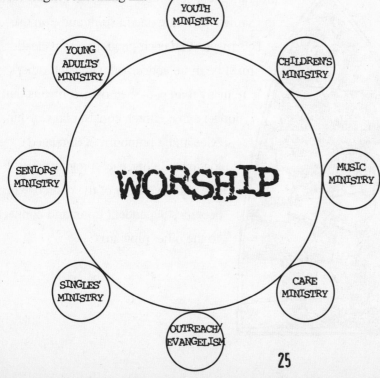

# What's the Answer?

The church's task is to create an environment in which Paul's words to the church at Philippi can take root:

> If you have any encouragement from being united with Christ, if any comfort from his love, if any fellowship with the Spirit, if any tenderness and compassion, then make my joy complete by being like-minded, having the same love, being one in spirit and purpose. Do nothing out of selfish ambition or vain conceit, but in humility consider others better than yourselves. Each of you should look not only to your own interests, but also to the interests of others. (Philippians 2:1–4)

For the church to be a community, a family of men, women, and children, of the elderly and the divorced, of the lonely and the seeking, then every program must commit to "being like-minded, having the same love, being one in spirit and purpose." This means that each program and its leadership must be more concerned with each other's ministry than with their own. It means that no longer can a church consist of a worship service and a potpourri of unrelated programs. Rather, each program must be drawn to the center of the church, where it becomes dependent upon and connected to the other programs.

# WHAT A CHURCH NEEDS TO FUNCTION AS A FAMILY

## 1. A unified vision of all programs

For a church to function as a family, it must be committed to a unified vision of every program and ministry. Church programs have evolved to the point that many now operate as parachurch programs within the context and under the umbrella of a local church. Perhaps this began with youth ministry, which a few decades ago modeled much of its programming after the successful pioneering work of Youth for Christ and Young Life in the 1950s and 1960s. Today nearly every ministry program in a local church operates as an independent entity. These programs vie for money, volunteers, and visibility as they attempt to carry out their ministries.

> All of the close, dynamic aspects of family life are to be found in the church body: cherishing, caring, encouraging, rebuking, confessing, repenting, confronting, forgiving, expressing kindness and communicating honestly.
>
> —*Charles Sell,* Family Ministry

Such an individualistic approach eventually harms families in a local church. Generations are segregated from one another. Children rarely sit with adults—if they attend worship services at all. Loyalists for each program and ministry squabble at board meetings and elsewhere around the church.

The church as Christ's body on earth must reverse this trend, remembering that we are all necessary to be a healthy community. Each program must see itself as a part of something bigger that God is doing. Every member of the body must be concerned about the other members. A unified vision for the local church is the first step in reshaping the church into God's family.

## 2. A commitment to people rather than to programs

The second thing that must occur for the local church to become a family-like community is for the leadership to adopt the attitude that the people God has drawn together are far more important than any program or ministry enterprise. Although most everyone would agree with this statement at a theoretical level, in practice, other people in the church often are viewed as obstacles to overcome or adversaries to be defeated.

The Scriptures couldn't be clearer on this. The night before Jesus was murdered, he told his best friends that the world would know who they are because of the love they had for each other (John 13:34-35). To Jesus there was nothing more important than love (Matthew 22:37-38). To Paul the gospel was summarized in that single word— love (Galatians 5:14). The Christian leader of today must heed these words, being absolutely convinced that God is far more concerned with how we treat one another than with how well our programs and ministries succeed.

# 3. A strategic calendar and program coordination

Only after both the lay and ordained leadership have committed to—

- creating a unified vision of all programs and ministries and

- agreeing to place personal relationships above programmatic or strategic priorities

will practical moves like calendar coordination make any difference. Once these two issues have been addressed, however, pragmatic and practical steps should be taken to ensure that the priorities of unity and vision are carried out. (See page 52 about a family-friendly church calendar.)

# 4. An intergenerational connection

If your church doesn't yet have an annual Youth Sunday, such an event may be a start toward intergenerational ministry—but it's only a start (and usually a paltry one at that). Because churches operate in varying demographics, intergenerational connectedness will look different from church to church. Here's what it *could* look like, though:

- A place for junior highers, senior highers, and college-age young adults on functioning church committees—and not merely as token students, observing only, but as contributing (though young) members of the church whose input around the table is considered.

> The church can be a family to families and a source of identity and support for isolated nuclear families—if it follows several principles:
> 1. It must be a place of diversity.
> 2. It must be a place where persons can get to know one another intimately.
> 3. It must create a role for all of its members.
> —*Jack O. Balswick and Judith K. Balswick, The Family*

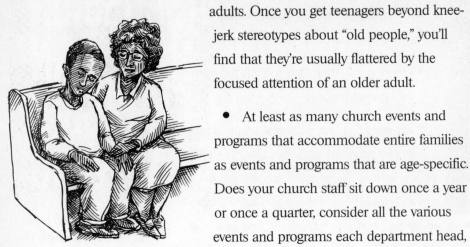

- As many middle-aged and older adults volunteering with the youth group as young adults. Once you get teenagers beyond knee-jerk stereotypes about "old people," you'll find that they're usually flattered by the focused attention of an older adult.

- At least as many church events and programs that accommodate entire families as events and programs that are age-specific. Does your church staff sit down once a year or once a quarter, consider all the various events and programs each department head, director, or associate pastor wants to do—and then ask the question, "How can we time, organize, and execute at least *half* of these events and programs in order to make them affairs that *all* church members can attend and enjoy together—single people, families (whether of infants, tots, or adolescents), single parents, seniors?"

The role of the pastoral staff in this notion of the church as a family of families takes on five functions:
- promote family integration
- encourage family adaptability
- facilitate family adjustment
- foster individuation
- develop community
—*Dennis Guernsey,* A New Design for Family Ministry

- High schoolers as regular members of the church choir.

The secret to making these ideas work is an unwavering commitment on the part of church leaders to an overall unified vision in which people's needs are the primary cause of concern, care, and prayer in the church.

# 9 Discussion Questions That Can Direct Your Church's Programming

The church of Jesus Christ is called to be a family, a people of God, and a vital community. What changes need to be made in your church in order to fully answer this call? Here are nine questions to discuss with others on your staff so that you may candidly assess your church's situation.

Sometimes your best planning tool can be your eraser.

—Tim Smith

## The Church As a Family

As apostles of Christ we could have been a burden to you, but we were gentle among you, like a mother caring for her little children. We loved you so much that we were delighted to share with you not only the gospel of God but our lives as well, because you had become so dear to us...For you know that we dealt with each of you as a father deals with his own children, encouraging, comforting and urging you to live lives worthy of God, who calls you into his kingdom and glory. (1 Thessalonians 2:7–8, 11–12)

**1.** Does your staff know and play with each

other—that is, does it try to model an extended family for the rest of the church?

**2.** Does every family unit in your church have a significant *spiritual* connection to at least two other families in the church?

**3.** During times of crisis as well as celebration, is there an authentic connection between people in your church? Do the people in your congregation really care for each other?

## The Church As the People of God

As a prisoner for the Lord, then, I urge you to live a life worthy of the calling you have received. Be completely humble and gentle; be patient, bearing with one another in love. Make every effort to keep the unity of the Spirit through the bond of peace. There is one body and one Spirit—just as you were called to one hope when you were called—one Lord, one faith, one baptism; one God and Father of all, who is over all and through all and in all. (Ephesians 4:1–6)

Wording, atmosphere, and attitude can make existing programs more effective.
—*Richard P. Olson and Joe H. Leonard, Jr.,* Ministry with Families in Flux

**4.** What is lord at your church—power, tradition, programs, or Jesus?

**5.** Are authentic relationships valued in your church as much as truth is?

**6.** Do your actions as a people—worship services, Sunday school classes, committees, missions—draw you closer to God?

## The Church as a Community

From him the whole body, joined and held together by every supporting ligament, grows and builds itself up in love, as each part does its work. So I tell you this, and insist on it in the Lord, that you must no longer live as the Gentiles do, in the futility of their thinking. They are darkened in their understanding and separated from the life of God because of the ignorance that is in them due to the hardening of their hearts. Having lost all sensitivity, they have given themselves over to sensuality so as to indulge in every kind of impurity, with a continual lust for more. (Ephesians 4:16–19)

**7.** Think of how your church's programs are planned and conducted. Do these programs encourage the building of relationships (both nuclear and intergenerational), merely tolerate them, or actually undermine them?

**8.** Are your church's expressions of community meaningful or merely cosmetic?

**9.** Do your church's people really know each other? Do they *want* to know each other?

> People desperately need community life as well as a rewarding family life. We must provide community life and meaningful fellowship for Christian families. That is part of being the family of God.
>
> —*Royce Money,*
> Ministering to Families

# FAMILY MINISTRY IN 5 CHURCHES

*Because family ministry means different things to different churches, no two of them will employ the same model of ministry. On the following pages you'll read how five churches define their ministry to families. These statements were written by the churches themselves.*

## Family Ministry at Meadow Park Church in Columbus, Ohio

The Board of Family Life Ministries was formed to provide a body within the organizational structure of Meadow Park Church that would act as an advocate for the family...that would initiate and support specific ministries to families both inside and outside the church membership.

Based on the belief, expressed by Marjorie Thompson in *Family, The Forming Center,* that "the family...is the foundational place of spiritual formation," the Board feels its priorities are to offer support, education, crisis intervention, and fellowship opportunities for many types of family units.

Family is a big word!

Family can mean—

- Traditional nuclear family

- Single parent with children

- Blended family (two parents
  with stepchildren)

- Single adult

- Traditional nuclear family with
  extended members

- Our own extended church family!

*(From promotional materials of Meadow Park Church,
Columbus, Ohio)*

# Marriage and Family Ministry at First Presbyterian Church in Margate, Florida

## *Purpose*
To implement a proactive resource ministry to build
strong Christ-centered individuals, couples and
families at First Presbyterian Church, local
communities and nationally, through an ongoing
equipping ministry to prepare individuals, couples
and families for each transitional stage of family life

and to provide, as may be necessary, key remedial ministries.

### *Focus of ministry*

- *Proactive (preventive) focus.* 70% of marriage and family ministry will be developing and implementing educational (short-term) and enrichment (long-term, six months to two years or more) programming.

- *Remedial focus.* 30% of the marriage and family ministry will be developing and implementing, as necessary, ongoing remedial (encouragement, confrontation, and support) programming.

*(From "Marriage and Family Ministry" by Dale Goodman of First Presbyterian Church, Margate, Florida)*

## Parent-Teen Ministry at Mariners South Coast Church in Irvine, California

*Mission statement.* To build healthy families by offering support, hope, training and God's grace to parents and their teens.

*Key verse.* "Except the Lord build the house, they labour in vain that build it: except the Lord keep the

It's no longer a question of *whether* I'll embrace a more family-focused approach to youth ministry. It's now just a question of how I'll do it.
—*Dave Rahn, "Parafamily Youth Ministry,"* Group Magazine

city, the watchman waketh but in vain. It is vain for you to rise up early, to sit up late, to eat the bread of sorrows: for so he giveth his beloved sleep. Lo, children are an heritage of the Lord: and the fruit of the womb is his reward. As arrows are in the hand of a mighty man; so are children of the youth. Happy is the man that hath his quiver full of them: they shall not be ashamed, but they shall speak with the enemies in the gate." (Psalm 127:1–5, KJV)

### Programs.

- *Workshops.* Six weeks, held on either Sunday mornings or Tuesday nights.

- *One-day specials.* Luau, Family Feud Night, Paint Ball Day.

- *"The Main Event."* Three-hour special seminars held once a month on either Friday nights or

Saturday mornings.

- *The Retreats.* "Manly Men Campout" for fathers and sons, family ski weekend in Utah, "Desert Retreat for the Fairer Sex."

*(From "Got Teens?" a publication of Mariners South Coast Church, Irvine, California)*

**The Family of the Future**
- Change will come slower.
- There will be more singles.
- The problem of POSSLQ (1980 Census Bureau's new category: People of Opposite Sex Sharing Living Quarters).
- There will be more one-parent families.
- The time for child bearing will be shortened.
- There will be longer "empty nests."
- There will be more older adults.

—*Dennis Guernsey*, A New Design for Family Ministry

# The Family of Believers at Highland Park Christian Church in Tulsa, Oklahoma

***Highland Park Christian Church is a family of believers.*** That expresses the premise of Family Ministry here at Highland Park. We believe that regardless of marital status or natural family relationships, each individual member of Highland Park is related to every other member by virtue of our adoption into God's family.

The purpose of Family Ministry at Highland Park is to strengthen families by helping them build deepening relationships with Christ and with one another. Our focus is on marriage and family issues. We offer support and training to help individual families within the church family relate to one another more effectively, to the end that they will ultimately model the nature of Jesus more completely. The outcome is *growth*—personal, family and corporate.

*(From the pamphlet "Allow Us to Introduce You to Our Family," by Highland Park Christian Church, Tulsa, Oklahoma)*

# Family Ministries at Grace Church in Edina, Minnesota

We at Grace Church are committed to the ministry of helping families in the vital process of their children growing in the grace and knowledge of the Lord Jesus Christ.

There are three assumptions we make in Family Ministries:

- Our mission is to *develop fully devoted followers of Jesus Christ.* We strive to do that in all aspects of the Family Ministries Division...We want families to grow in their relationship to Christ.

- *People take priority over programs.* Our family ministry begins with getting to know you as individual families and from that starting point, we seek to help you develop in your relationship with

God, with your spouse and with your children.

- *Families are a priority.* We are committed to helping you and your family in specific ways. That is why we have a large staff who want to be of assistance to you in any way possible.

*(From the family ministries brochure of Grace Church, Edina, Minnesota)*

# CREATING A SUCCESSFUL FAMILY MINISTRY

# 4 Options for Integrating Youth and Family Ministries

## 1. Family-friendly youth ministry

Although in this model family ministry is the responsibility of the church-at-large, the youth ministry makes a conscious effort to program in a way that demonstrates awareness of and sensitivity to the issues families face—including money, busyness, and spending time together.

## 2. Family-focused youth ministry

This model entails what Dave Rahn of Huntington College calls the "slash approach" to programming—father/son, mother/daughter, brother/sister. Yet at least it's a move away from youth-focused ministry events and toward intergenerational ministry (especially within the nuclear family setting). In this setup the ultimate responsibility for family ministry remains outside the youth ministry program, but the youth ministry devotes a significant amount of time and energy to family programs.

# 3. Youth-focused family ministry

This model is a shift in both thinking and programming. According to this perspective, the purpose of the youth ministry is to support what God does in and through the home. The youth minister (and staff) equip parents and youths to foster an environment of spiritual maturity and training within the context of the family system.

# 4. Youth-friendly family ministry

From a historical youth ministry framework, this is the most radical model of all. Essentially, the family is the key target and ministry focus of the entire church. The assumption is that if the family is being strengthened, then so are the adolescents within that family.

Okay, so which approach is best? It is the responsibility of individual churches to decide which approach will best meet the specific needs of their congregation. Every situation is unique; every church faces constant change. Demographic issues, expectations, growth, resources, and facilities must be carefully considered before a model of youth-and-family ministry is chosen.

*(Adapted from "Parafamily Youth Ministry" by Dave Rahn, in* Group Magazine, *May/June 1996)*

**Ways families need to be strengthened:**
- Healthy communication
- Affirmation, support, and appreciation
- Sense of trust, mutual respect, and shared responsibility
- Develop a sense of commitment
- Time together
- Spiritual convictions and values
- Reaching out to others
  —*Royce Money,* Ministering to Families

# Questions to Ask as You Contemplate a Move into Family-Friendly Youth Ministry

Thinking about adding a family emphasis to your youth ministry? Ask yourself (and your staff) these questions before you choose a course of action:

• What are we doing now for only the youth that we can modify to become more family friendly?

• How can we naturally connect kids with their parents and siblings?

• What are we doing now that we could lose in order to add more family-friendly programs?

• In what ways are we unintentionally hurting families in our church? (See "If You Want to Hurt a Family, Do This," on page 95.)

• How far can we push our congregation toward family ministry now? How far will we be able to push them in the next three to six months? Where do we want to be two years from now?

**Keep accurate family records.**
Regularly check the accuracy of your list of students' first and last names, including hyphenated names, international names, and multiple surnames. For kids whose parents are divorced or separated, keep accurate records of both parents—even those out of state. Be sure to send both parents any material that goes out.

Family Not-so-friendly

Family Friendly

# 7 STEPS TOWARD FAMILY-BASED YOUTH MINISTRY

**Supporting single parents.**
In *Ministry with Families in Flux,* Richard Olson and Joe Leonard suggest that every church should somehow provide three levels of support for single parents:
• *Formal support* that offers (or at least provides referrals for) services ranging from professional therapeutic counseling to crisis intervention.
• *Informal support,* consisting of individual help and opportunities for group help, whether for single parents exclusively, or in broader settings in which single parents feel welcomed and comfortable.
• *Informal connections* across all generations in the church. The research of Olson and Leonard notes that "in fact single parents seek most the informal support of friends and groups."

## 1. Start slow.

The baby-steps approach is the best way for both individuals and the church to understand and accept this new movement.

## 2. Enlist support before you begin.

Change is rarely easy; many people actively resist it. Before you make a move, get several others on board so that the move is a well-considered, team shift.

## 3. Plan for the little things.

Issues such as timing, transportation, money, and child care all need to be considered when it comes to family ministry programs.

## 4. Develop a calendar-sensitive mentality.

A problem many churches have is that the various ministries have no idea how their programs affect other ministries. Make sure that someone is responsible for overseeing the entire church calendar to ensure that the church as a whole is family friendly. (See "The Family-Friendly Church Calendar" on page 52.)

# 5. Be committed before you begin.

The shift to a family-based youth ministry is not a programmatic move you can merely try out for a while. The commitment to a family emphasis must represent a fundamental change in how, why, and with whom you do ministry. If such a shift is ever to work, it must be acknowledged that there is no turning back.

# 6. Take a calculated risk implementing new, untraditional, or even wacko ideas.

A commitment to family-friendly youth ministry presents an opportunity to try out all kinds of new programming ideas. Somebody had to be the first to try a junior high lock-in.

**Planning for family ministry** (one approach):
1. Define the problem.
2. State the objectives.
3. Identify constraints to possible solutions.
4. List several possible solutions.
5. Tentatively select the most feasible solution.
6. Identify key people who should be involved in the next step.
7. List the steps or activities that the proposed solution will entail.
8. Set a schedule for such activities.
9. Identify the resources that will be needed.
10. Have a plan to evaluate and modify.
—*Royce Money*, Ministering to Families

# 7. Look for ways to take something old and make it new.

Most programs become stale when people simply do what they have always done before. Some of the most creative ministry ideas involve revitalizing a worn-out idea by adding a twist to it.

# ESTABLISHING A FAMILY MINISTRY COMMITTEE

A family ministry committee can be an effective tool in helping a church become more family friendly. Here's what such a committee looks like:

The words of Jesus "Be as shrewd as snakes and innocent as doves" aptly describe the ideal members of a family ministry committee. So look for people who are not only influential, but godly and gentle as well. If the members of the committee are godly but relationally meek, they will be fun to work with but may not accomplish much. If they are politically influential but have serious, ongoing, unresolved spiritual questions or issues, the committee may cause more relational problems than it solves.

- It is composed of five to eight people.

- It should include a representative from each of the major ministries of the church, if possible.

- It includes the decision makers of the church's various ministries.

- It includes people who are more interested in the church as a whole than they are about their own program or ministry.

- It includes people who are willing to love one another as a prerequisite for making programmatic decisions.

- It reflects the demographic as well as programmatic makeup of your church.

- Ironic as it seems, busy people usually make the best members of a family ministry committee. More often than not, busy people are busy because they care and have the ability to get things done. If you recruit busy people, of course, make sure the meetings are organized and to-the-point.

- Distribute an agenda at least a week before the meeting so that members can determine how they feel about a certain issue and do their homework.

- Members of a family ministry committee get to know each other—and each other's—arena within the church. The committee meetings themselves should be only the tip of the relational iceberg.

# DEALING WITH RESISTANCE

Churchgoers may favor the idea of family ministry, but are not at all sure what is meant by the term. As a result when you try to implement even the most innocuous program to move a church or organization toward a family-friendly focus, it is possible, even likely, that you will encounter resistance—or at least nervousness about programmatic or philosophical change. So how should you deal with it?

> Even if you're on the right track, you'll get run over if you just sit there.
>
> —*Will Rogers*

• Enlist a prayer team, or at least one prayer warrior,

Hey, not bad!

FAMILY MINISTRY

who will commit to praying about the shift to family ministry.

- Identify *where* the resistance is coming from and *why*. Do not allow a nonissue to become an issue.

- Try not to worry too much about turf and territory, but rather be a servant to those ministries and people who may feel threatened by any potential changes.

- The lay people who do share your vision for family ministry should be handed as much leadership and ownership of the ministry as possible. They will be your greatest sales force.

- Speak the language of the church leadership. If you use buzz words, use buzz words your church understands and is comfortable with.

- Give them a taste of the cookie. (This was, incidentally, the slogan for a Nabisco marketing campaign to obtain shelf space at grocery stores.) Let detractors experience family ministry firsthand— but make sure it's a good taste!

- Implement change slowly, in bite-sized portions.

A great many people think they are thinking when they are only rearranging their prejudices.
—*William James*

We should be careful to get out of an experience only the wisdom that is in it—and stop there; lest we be like the cat that sits down on a hot stove lid. She will never sit down on a hot stove lid again—and that is well, but also she will never sit down on a cold one anymore.
—*Mark Twain*

# THE FAMILY-FRIENDLY CHURCH CALENDAR

Of all things, the calendar can be a potent enemy of a church's family-friendliness. As ministries grow and leaders get busy trying to do all that is required of them, independent programming begins surfacing again. As clergy and laypersons try to find time to get together to make wise and timely decisions, it is hard enough to coordinate the calendars of the individual program's leadership staff, much less work through the schedule of the entire church. Yet coordinating schedules is a necessary step in creating a family-like church community.

Calendar coordination will be successful and helpful only when two initial ingredients are present:

- A unified vision of *all* ministries and programs throughout the church.
- A commitment of the entire church leadership to a philosophy that values people over program. (See "What a Church Needs to Function as a Family," page 27.)

Here are some ground rules to consider as a staff as you're coordinating the church calendar:

To support blended families, schedule major educational and fellowship activities of the church on a weeknight. This recognizes that children from blended families or single-parent homes may be visiting the other parent on weekends. The *way* church activities are promoted and carried out is often more important in ministry with changing families than adding a special program for a particular family type.
— *Richard Olson and Joe Leonard,*
Ministry with Families in Flux

**1.** A regular meeting will be held weekly (or more often, if necessary) to go over the calendar requests and make recommendations to a person (or group of people) in a leadership position. This may be a church administrator, senior pastor, head elder, or a body of leaders. This person (or group) will make final calendar decisions based upon the input from the staff members or lay people making the requests.

**2.** Once established, the calendar will be changed only after all affected parties and leaders responsible for the calendar have been given ample time to consider the request and the implications of the change.

**3.** Although one person manages the calendar, no one person, regardless of position, tenure, or salary, may override the calendar.

**4.** No calendar decision is official until it has gone through the proper channels.

Following these guidelines may be difficult for many churches at first, but in time they will become a tremendous help in maintaining a commitment to a unified vision and a philosophy that emphasizes people over program.

> We are not defining family ministry as simply more programs for families…. We see the fundamental role of congregations as sources of family support and the role of church leaders as coordinators of that support.
> —*Richard Olson and Joe Leonard,*
> *Ministry with Families in Flux*

# Involving Moms & Dads in Family Ministry

3

# 13 WAYS TO START INVOLVING PARENTS IN YOUTH MINISTRY

Would you like the parents of your youth group members to become a more integral part of your ministry? Consider the following list of suggestions:

**1.** Recruit a parent council. (See the next chapter.)

**2.** Schedule quarterly parent meetings. (See page 61.)

**3.** Publish a regular parent newsletter. (See page 64.)

**4.** Start a parents prayer ministry. (See page 76.)

**5.** Socialize among your students' parents. (See page 66.)

**6.** Make sure that your youth ministry calendar is family friendly. (See page 52.)

**7.** Conduct a parent survey. (There's one you can

In my mind a truly cooperative church does more than provide seminars on family-related topics, however basic they may be. A cooperative church defines its role in such a way that it genuinely serves its members by actively strengthening their families.
—*Dennis Guernsey*, A New Design for Family Ministry

use as-is on page 104.)

**8.** Develop a parent resource library. (See pages 70–76.)

**9.** Curtail expenses for your youth group activities and events.

THANKS FOR USING "DAD the ATM."

**10.** Celebrate the parents of your youth group members. (See page 68.)

**11.** Encourage your group members' parents whenever you see them.

**12.** Use parents as teachers for your youth group.

**13.** Put together a family ministry committee. (See page 48.)

**Watch the bucks!**

It can be expensive to be the parent of a youth ministry kid! Whether it is for lunch and a movie following church ($13), a new T-shirt ($13), a ticket for a concert ($13), or a spring break missions trip ($313), parents are constantly being asked to fork over more and more money so their kids can attend youth group events. In a family ministry setting the problem is compounded because more family members are involved. One church held its annual three-night family camp at a mountain retreat at a cost of $650 for a family of five. (That's well beyond the budget of most families of five I know.)

Expenses like these can be extremely hard on families. Parents want their kids to be involved, yet they feel the financial crunch. To be family friendly, Christian leaders must consider the hard costs of programming, and then create ways to reduce the financial load on parents and families.

# DEVELOPING A PARENT COUNCIL

One of the most important aspects of an effective family-centered youth ministry is a functioning parent council. As you set about creating a parent council, consider these tips:

• Include a variety of people on the council— parents of high school students, parents of middle schoolers, parents of a few younger kids who will be moving up soon, and even parents of former students.

• Meet monthly.

• Always start and end meetings on time.

• Appoint a parent to run meetings of the parent council. You and your youth ministry staff should participate in the meetings, not lead them. Meet with the chairperson before each meeting to plan the agenda, which may include updates of past events and ministry as well as the planning and discussion of upcoming events.

• Ensure that the parent council has clear ownership of future events. It shouldn't exist to merely rubber-stamp your program. An effective parent council can help you think through all

Research continues to show that, for better or for worse, a teen's family represents the most influential network of earthly relationships in his or her life. For this simple reason, we believe that the most effective youth ministry always takes place in the context of the family.
—*Tom Lytle, Kelly Schwartz, Gary Hartke,* 101 Ways to Be Family-Friendly in Youth Ministry

aspects of your ministry—from programs to finances to overall vision.

• Thank the council members—tangibly—at least once a year. That means a gift of some sort. Regular cards, notes, and phone calls of appreciation will also go a long way in establishing rapport with your council members.

• Socialize with members individually in order to get to know them and let them know that you appreciate their involvement.

# CHECKLIST FOR A PERFECT PARENT MEETING

Parent meetings may be important, but they aren't necessarily fun. Yet they can become a highlight among a youth ministry staff. The following suggestions are intended to help you plan and execute painless and productive parent meetings.

☑ Is the entire youth ministry staff present—dressed for parents—before the first parent arrives?

☑ Is coffee and other "adult food" ready before people arrive?

☑ Is the meeting room well lit, with chairs arranged in an orderly fashion, posters of ministry photos placed around the room, and upbeat music playing softly?

☑ Does the meeting start on time and last no longer than an hour? Did you make this an advertising point before the meeting?

☑ Does a well-known and respected parent run the meeting? Did she or he meet with the youth ministry leaders ahead of time to set an agenda?

☑ Does the agenda relect the goals for a parent

For years now, in survey after survey, parents emerge as the undisputed, unbeaten, and untied champions of spiritual impact on kids' lives. No one, no matter how mega-riffic their ministry, makes more of a difference in kids' spiritual growth than their parents.

Yet it is as if the church has given up on parents as spiritual leaders for their young people. We create programs and ministries designed to usurp, not fuel, parents as spiritual trainers. We've communicated that the church, not the home, is the best place for young people to find encouragement and accountability in their journey with God.

—Rick Lawrence, "Looking Forward," Group Magazine

meeting: to inform, encourage, and equip parents?

☑ Does the meeting elicit the support and allegiance of parents? (Parental support comes when they're convinced that the youth staff knows what it is doing, that it takes its job and kids seriously, and that it cares about the needs and issues of parents and families in general.)

☑ Do you take advantage of parent meetings—especially immediately before and after the meeting itself—to talk personally with parents, affirming them and their child?

☑ Is information presented creatively and in such a way that parents don't feel like they've wasted their time by attending the meeting? For example, don't merely announce the dates and cost of summer camp, but instead give parents two or three options to consider as a group—summer camp being only one of the options—or else sell the camp and its cost so that the majority will be excited with you about the event. A student's brief testimony about last summer's camp followed by a brief video can help you do this. In any case, get parental input before you commit to a course of action—and a parent meeting is the perfect place for this type of discussion. Plus the parents who don't come to the meeting can't blame your staff for decisions *parents* made at the meeting.

✔ Do most parent meetings include at least a few words if not a workshop by a parenting expert or adolescent pyschologist? Invite a local school official, a family therapist, a youth or family minister from another church or organization, or a local political figure. Publicize the speaker's appearance before the meeting, keep the speaker to 20 minutes or so, and compensate him or her appropiately.

✔ Does the youth staff stay and mingle until the last parent leaves? (If you do, then you can finish off the refreshments.)

# THE PARENT NEWSLETTER

**1.** Today's families are busier than ever. Parents need to know what's going on well in advance so they can plan accordingly.

**2.** Most parents rely on the youth program to develop a sense of spirituality in their kids. They may recognize their own primary responsibility for their kids' spiritual well-being, but they also need all the help they can get. A newsletter lets them know that the youth program is on top of that need.

**3.** Parents need encouragement about their kids. A word from people who work directly with their kids means a great deal.

**4.** In the rush of life, "out of sight, out of mind" has never been truer. A monthly newsletter reminds parents of the value of the youth ministry program.

The best way to help parents feel that they are part of your ministry is to publish a quarterly (or even monthly) newsletter for them. If your mailing costs get out of hand, distribute the students' newsletter at youth ministry events and spend your budget on the parents' newsletter.

## What Should a Parent Newsletter Do?

### • *Inform*

Parents do not appreciate calendars or cute clip art; as much as they do *lists!* Well in advance of an event—especially a major event or one that costs money, like a camp or retreat—parents should know the date and cost of the event. Each newsletter should include the times and locations for every youth ministry event in the next two months, as well as the phone numbers of the entire youth ministry staff.

### • *Encourage*

Parents can be nervous when it comes to their teenagers. They need to be reminded that the church or parachurch leadership recognizes that parenting is difficult and nerve-racking. So include somewhere in your newsletter at least a paragraph that lets parents know that they are appreciated and that you understand what they're going through. A touch like this reminds parents that you're on their side.

## • *Equip*

Parents tend to resent youth workers, paid or not, who come across like they know kids better than the parents do. Yet at the same time, youth workers *can* provide insight that helps parents be more effective. A quote from a youth expert, family counselor, or educator lets parents know that you and the youth staff can be a resource for them whenever needed.

## Practical Matters

• Keep your parent newsletter short, or it won't be read.

• Use a large font—at least 12- or 14-point type.

• Make the layout attractive, simple, and easy to follow.

• Regularly ask for feedback from parents, then convert that feedback into changes in subsequent issues.

• Invite a few parents to head up the newsletter production and mailing.

• Keep the tone of the newsletter light, fun, and warm.

# KNOW THE PARENTS BEHIND YOUR YOUTH GROUP

How do youth leaders cultivate relationships with the parents of students?

**1.** Make a point to get on a first-name basis with most, if not all, of the parents of the kids in your group.

**2.** Don't be the constant bearer of bad news. Instead learn to specifically compliment parents on their kids every time you see them.

Without parental support, the likelihood of a teen continuing in the faith as an adult is reduced significantly.
—Wayne Rice, in *Tag Team Youth Ministry* by Ron Habermas and David Olshine

**3.** Do contact work with the parents of your group members. Talk to them at games, recitals, plays, and other events that you are both attending. Divide your time between the kids and the adults at such events.

**4.** Make a point to get especially close to two or three families from your group. Allow these people to help you understand the issues you need to work on as a leader.

**5.** Whenever you see or run into a parent, drop that person a note within two days, thanking him for taking the time to talk. If you agreed on anything—changing the date of an event, attending a youth program as your guest—mention that as well.

**6.** Send individual parents cards from time to time, encouraging them and expressing your appreciation for the job they are doing in raising their kids.

**7.** Identify the single-parent families in your group. When you see these parents, ask if there is any way you (or your ministry) could be of service to them.

**8.** Make a point of asking parents, "What can I do for you?"

The interviews I have had with men in their thirties and forties convince me that the psychological or physical absence of fathers from their families is one of the great underestimated tragedies of our times. I believe there is considerable sense of loss hidden within men, having to do with their fathers.
*—Samuel Osherson,*
Finding Our Fathers

# 13 WAYS TO CELEBRATE PARENTS

Parents are vital to your ministry. Take advantage of every opportunity you have to build relationships with them. What kind of opportunities, you ask?

Parents should function as midwives for the birth of spirituality in our children. A midwife does not drag the baby from the mother's womb, but assists the mother in her own work of giving birth. So too, we must gently guide and lead, only interfering when the health of the spiritual baby is in jeopardy. Kids, like all of us, stick with decisions that are their own better than they do with those that are forced upon them.
—*Terry W. Glaspey,* Children of a Greater God

**1** Write them a note to thank them for their child.

**2** Stop them in the halls at church and pay them a compliment.

**3.** Highlight one parent, couple, or family in every parent newsletter.

**4.** Give parents a gift at Christmas.

**5.** Have students put on a "Celebrate Our Parents" evening, complete with music, skits, and a time when some of them, at least, can sit on their parents' laps and present them with handmade gifts.

**6.** Send parents a cake on their wedding anniversary.

**7.** Take them to lunch on their birthday.

**8.** Call them to ask how you can pray for them.

**9.** Meet with them once a semester to get their advice on how to best help their child grow in Christ.

**10.** See them as partners.

**11.** Seek out their advice.

**12.** Brag about them to their kids.

**13.** Provide free babysitting services once a month.

# CREATING A PARENT RESOURCE LIBRARY

As you move toward a family-friendly youth ministry, you'll need to update your resource library. The following books and articles are ideal resources not only for your youth ministry staff, but for parents as well. Establishing a parent resource library will go a long way toward involving your kids' moms and dads in your ministry.

- *As Iron Sharpens Iron,* Howard Hendricks and William Hendricks (Moody Press, 1995).

- *Boys to Men: How Fathers Can Help Build Character in Their Sons,* Steve Lee and Chap Clark (Moody Press, 1995).

- *Bridges,* Mark DeVries and Nan Russell (InterVarsity Press, 1996).

- *A Call to Family Reformation: Restoring the Soul of America One Home at a Time,* Dennis Rainey (Family Life, 1994).

- *Caring That Enables: A Manual for Developing Parish Family Ministry,* Leif Kehrwald (Paulist Press, 1991).

- *Children of a Greater God,* Terry W. Glaspey (Harvest House, 1995).

- *The Church's Ministry with Families,* Diana Garland and Diane Pancoast (eds.) (Word, 1990).

- ***The Coming Revolution in Youth Ministry,*** Mark Senter (Victor, 1992).

- ***Community That Is Christian,*** Julie Gorman (Victor Books, 1993).

- ***Complete Handbook for Family Life Ministry in the Church,*** Don Hebbard (Nelson, 1995).

- ***Effective Christian Education: A National Study of Protestant Congregations—A Summary Report on Faith, Loyalty, and Congregational Life,*** Peter L. Benson and Carolyn H. Elkin (Search Institute, 1990).

- ***Families at the Crossroads: Beyond Traditional and Modern Options,*** Rodney Clapp (InterVarsity Press, 1994).

- ***Families Growing Together: Church Programs for Family Living,*** Scott M. Miles (Victor, 1990).

- ***The Family: A Christian Perspective on the Contemporary Home,*** Jack O. Balswick and Judith K. Balswick (Baker, 1989).

- ***Family-Based Youth Ministry,*** Mark DeVries (InterVarsity Press, 1994).

- ***Family Building: Six Qualities of a Strong Family,*** George Rekers (ed.) (Regal, 1985).

- ***Family-Centered Church,*** Gerald Foley (Sheed & Ward, 1995).

- ***The Family-Friendly Church,*** Richard D. Dobbins (Creation House, 1989).

- ***Family Ministry*** (Second Edition), Charles M. Sell (Zondervan, 1995).

- ***Finding Our Fathers: The Unfinished Business of Manhood,*** Samuel Osherson

(Free Press, 1986).

- ***The Five Cries of Parents,*** Merton Strommen and Irene Strommen (Harper & Row, 1985).

- ***Five Key Habits of Smart Dads,*** Paul Lewis (Zondervan, 1996).

- ***The Future of the American Family,*** George Barna (Moody Press, 1993).

- ***Helping Teens in Crisis,*** Miriam Neff (Tyndale, 1993).

- ***Like Dew Your Youth: Growing Up with Your Teenager,*** Eugene Peterson (Eerdmans, 1994).

- ***Ministering to Families: A Positive Plan of Action,*** Royce Money (Abilene Christian University, 1987).

- ***Ministry with Families in Flux: The Church and Changing Patterns of Life,*** Richard P. Olson and Joe H. Leonard, Jr. (Westminster/John Knox, 1990).

- ***Mothers and Daughters Making Peace: The Most Intimate, Tangled, Beautiful, & Frustrating Relationship Shared by Women,*** Judith K. Balswick (Servant, 1993).

- ***A New Design for Family Ministry,*** Dennis Guernsey (David C. Cook, 1992).

- ***101 Ways to Be Family-Friendly in Youth Ministry,*** Tom Lytle, Kelly Schwartz, and Gary Hartke (Beacon Hill, 1996).

- ***130 Ways to Involve Parents in Youth Ministry,*** (Group Books, 1994).

- ***Parenting Adolescents*** (video curriculum), Kevin Huggins (NavPress, 1989).

- ***Past, Present, and Personal: The Family and the Life Course in America,*** John Demos (Oxford University Press, 1986).

- ***Rebuilding the Nest: A New Commitment to the American Family,*** David Blankenhorn (ed.) (Harvest House, 1990).

- ***The Relaxed Parent: Helping Your Kids Do More As You Do Less,*** Tim Smith (Northfield, 1996).

- ***Saving Your Marriage Before It Starts,*** Les and Leslie Parrott (Zondervan, 1995).

- ***Seven Secrets of Highly Effective Fathers,*** Ken Canfield, (Tyndale, 1992).

- ***The Shelter of Each Other: Rebuilding Our Families,*** Mary Pipher (Ballantine, 1996).

- ***Silence of Adam,*** Larry Crabb (Zondervan, 1995).

- ***Sociology of the Family,*** Steven L. Nock (Prentice-Hall, 1987).

- ***Tag-Team Youth Ministry: 50 Practical Ways to Involve Parents and Other Caring Adults,*** Ronald Habermas and David Olshine (Standard, 1995).

- ***There's a New Family in My House! Blending Stepfamilies Together,*** Laura Walters (Harold Shaw, 1993).

- ***Traits of a Healthy Family,*** Dolores Curran (Winston Press, 1983).

- ***Understanding Today's Youth Culture,*** Walter Mueller (Tyndale, 1994).

- ***Understanding Your Teenager*** (video Curriculum) Wayne Rice (Youth Specialties, 1992).

# PARENT-RESOURCE ORGANIZATIONS

As part of your parent resource library (see the previous chapter), you should have on file the names and addresses of parachurch organizations dedicated to family ministry and parent training. Because of organizational turnover, you should probably update this file at least once a year. The following list of organizations should provide a starting point for you:

> The church's strategy should include finding means for the family to discover companionship and help outside itself.
>
> —*Charles Sell,* Family Ministry

- **Center for Parent/Youth Understanding, P.O. Box 414, Elizabethtown, PA 17022 (717-361-8429)** Walt Mueller, president of this organization, is nationally recognized as a leader in training and equipping parents, especially in terms of culture and media issues. The CPYU publishes an excellent quarterly newsletter for parents and youth workers, and also sponsors seminars and training events for churches, schools, and other youth organizations.

- **Family Information Services, 12565 Jefferson Street NE, Suite 102, Minneapolis, MN 55434-2102 (familyinfo@aol.com)** The mission of FIS is "to bring the messages of love, respect, responsibility, and hope from Scripture to the practical application level in order to aid families in creating a healthy family environment that is conducive to growing in faith, and where parents and children can reach their full potential in Christ."

- **FamilyLife, P.O. Box 23840, Little Rock, AR 72221 (800-333-1433)** FamilyLife offers both weekend marriage and parenting conferences. The organization also offers "The Family Manifesto," a comprehensive statement on the definition and functioning of the family.

- **Family Works, Board of Christian Education of the Church of God, P.O. Box 2458, Anderson, IN 46018-2458** This denominational organization offers new ministry resources for family advocates.

- **Focus on the Family, 8605 Explorer Drive, Colorado Springs, CO 80920 (719-531-5181)** *Single-Parent Family* magazine, published by Focus on the Family, encourages and helps single parents to maintain a sense of familial stability. Contributing authors include Gary Oliver, Bill Butterworth, John Townsend, and Henry Cloud.

- **Kids Hope, 189 Illini Drive, Woodland Park, CO 80863 (719-687-0515)** The mission of Kids Hope is "to reach children whose birth-parents are divorced, separated, widowed or never married, by showing them that trouble can turn to Hope... The methods for ministry are instruction, video presentation, learning activities, music, small group

discussion." Kids Hope offers seminars for children, youth, and leadership training.

- **Legacy Family Ministries (Byron and Carla Weathersbee), P.O. Box 20324, Waco, TX 76702-0234 (817-772-0412)** "Planting relationships that will last forever," this organization runs family camps, training seminars, and classes dealing with family, parenting, and marriage issues.

- **The Northwest Fathering Forum, 15600 Redmond Way, Suite 200, Redmond, WA 98052 (206-883-0208)** The purpose of this forum is to "equip fathers in the Northwest through inspiration, instruction and intercession." Activities include monthly meetings, fathering groups, and parenting classes.

- **Today's Family, 1482 Lakeshore Drive, Branson, MO 65616 (800-84TODAY)** Gary Smalley's popular Love Is a Decision seminars address several practical issues: "Emotional Word Pictures: How to Communicate," "Finding Fulfillment," and "How to Establish Healthy Boundaries." These two-day seminars are designed for "married couples, singles, engaged couples, pastors, and anyone from 18 to 80" who want "their relationships to be the best they can be."

**Moms-of-Teens** is a prayer ministry of the youth program at Cherry Creek Presbyterian Church in Englewood, Colorado. The group's role is to uphold the youth department and students active in the youth group, meeting weekly to pray for the church's teens and its youth ministry.

There's also **Moms in Touch,** a North America-wide program calling for Christian mothers from various churches to gather in homes and pray for their schools. Getting parents to pray for students in the community as well as in the church raises consciousness and sensitivity toward young people.

# PROGRAMMING YOUR FAMILY MINISTRY

# FAMILY ACTIVITIES FOR THE WHOLE CHURCH

## Family Mission Trips

These may be either short-term (weekend) trips or longer (lasting a week or more) excursions, giving families and individuals the opportunity to experience mission work firsthand.

## Father-Child and Mother-Child Retreats

Fathers or mothers and children of any age are given an opportunity to take a day or two together to celebrate their relationship.

## Prom Night

Everybody is invited to this gala event, which includes music from all eras, tons of food, and lively entertainment. Attendees should dress in the style of the year they graduated (or will graduate) from high school.

## Serve-a-Thon

Members of the church, regardless of age, come together on a Saturday to serve either

> Single people—whether divorced, never married, or widowed—need a functional family relationship. The church is uniquely equipped for this purpose. Perhaps the greatest ministry the church has to singles is to provide for them a functional, spiritual family-like atmosphere.
> —*Royce Money*, Ministering to Families

The ingredients common to most strong families appear to include—

- Strong, supportive, honest communication
- A significant quantity of time spent together
- Shared religious faith and practice
- Agreement on key values
- Love, consideration, understanding, mutual appreciation
- Common interests, goals, purposes
- Ability to positively negotiate solutions to crises
- Commitment to deepening the intrafamily relationships
- Optimism about the stability of the family
- A firm parental coalition in dealing with children
- Regular sexual intercourse with the spouse
- Willingness to sacrifice personal interest and resources for the good of the family
- Behavior that earns the trust of the family members.

—*George Barna,* The Future of the American Family

members of the church in need (such as widows or shut-ins) or the community. Children will have the opportunity to work alongside grandparents. This may be a quarterly (or even monthly) event.

## My Favorite Movie

Once a quarter (or so) plan a family movie night. Have the different age groups take turns deciding what movie will be shown on a given night. During intermission encourage a few people from the age group that chose the movie explain why it is a favorite of theirs and what they remember about it. Whether the movie is *Sabrina, The Great Escape,* or *The Princess Bride,* this event cannot help but draw the church family together.

# CREATIVE FAMILY CAMPS

A camp setting offers a variety of bonding opportunities for kids and parents. In order to take advantage of the unique possibilities family camps offer, you'll need to consider the following tips:

• Hold as many meetings as you can as a group. Separate the age groups as little as possible.

• Incorporate as much audience participation as you can, using children primarily, but not exclusively. Do not allow the "elders" to sit back and avoid participation.

• Have each age group prepare and present a drama that fits the message or theme of each meeting.

• Use as much creative media as possible. Incorporate arts and crafts, Play-Doh, clippings from newspapers and magazines, old movies, clips from TV shows, songs, tape-recorded sounds, and anything else you can think of into your meetings.

• Use competition to integrate the age groups. Make the games fun, but easy enough for everyone to participate in.

- Keep a balance between active and passive elements in every meeting. Use singing, small groups, mixers, and other ideas to keep people moving around.

- Give every family a cassette tape of the songs you will be singing at the camp to listen to on the way to camp.

- Hand every family a sealed envelope to be opened as soon as they leave town on their way to camp. In it, provide some instructions to be followed during the trip to camp. These instructions might include things like preparing a family skit to perform, playing a game together, and discussing an issue that will be brought up at camp.

- Put your money into a facility, a speaker, and a musician that can facilitate what you want to accomplish. Many groups attempt to put on an entire camp themselves. Recognize that the church's leaders need a break as much as the congregation does. Fresh perspectives from gifted, seasoned resource people will enhance the camp experience for everyone.

# WORKSHOPS THAT WORK

## Parenting

For better or worse, parenting is usually learned through trial and error. Any help that you and your ministry could provide through informal parenting classes benefits not only parents, but their children—and ultimately your ministry. Consider these topics for a parenting seminar at your church:

- Developing capable kids: A workshop on building a child's self-esteem

- Teens to parents: Kids teach their parents about current issues

- Winning your kids back from the media

- Preparation for parenting: A workshop for expectant parents

- Preparing for the school years

- The art of parental discipline throughout a child's life

The church needs to be educated about changing families; families need to be educated about their responsibilities and opportunities.
—*Richard P. Olson and Joe H. Leonard, Jr.,* Ministry with Families in Flux

- Parental wisdom from proverbs

- Parenting junior highers

- Parenting when it's almost too late: The art of being a parent of high schoolers

- Preparing for college: Transitional parenting

- Raising adolescents alone: Single parenting

- What worked (and what didn't work) for us: Empty-nesters share their parenting history

- Fathering daughters through adolescence

- Fathering sons through adolescence

- Is "Christian athlete" an oxymoron? The role of sports in a Christian family

- Developing rites of passage

- Dealing with hyperactive or difficult kids

## Stepparenting in particular

If parenting is one of the hardest jobs in the world, stepparenting can only be harder. Most stepparents are unequipped for the tasks they face, so they appreciate any help you and your ministry can offer them in the form of training seminars. Here are some ideas for stepparenting classes you might consider:

- Understanding the unique problems of stepparenting

- Understanding the unique potential of a stepparent

- The stepchild's world

- The myth of instant love

- Discipline in a stepfamily

- Dealing with the nonresident parent

A man approached a laborer who was laying bricks and asked, "What are you doing?" The laborer replied, "Can't you see I'm laying bricks?" The man then walked over to another bricklayer and asked, "What are you doing?" And the workman answered with pride, "I am building a cathedral."

Physically they were both doing the same thing. But the first laborer was occupied with the present task, while the other had in mind the ultimate goal.

—*Larry Anderson*, Taking the Trauma Out of Teen Transitions

• The importance of the marriage in a stepfamily

# Parent-Teen Classes

A particularly effective way to introduce a family emphasis into your youth ministry is to conduct occasional classes that parents and their teenagers attend together. The following is a list of subjects you might consider addressing in these classes:

• Sex and dating

• Choosing a mate

• Money, time, and fun

• Being a friend

• Learning how to communicate

• My needs and your needs

• Making decisions

• Family prayer

• Studying the Bible

• Movies, MTV, and music: How to handle the media

---

**A One-Day Parenting Seminar for All Ages and Seasons of Life**

Most churches try to hit issues specific to an age group or parenting season—new family, teens in the house, empty nesters, etc.

Instead try a one-day parenting seminar for *all* ages and seasons. The schedule could look something like this:

| | |
|---|---|
| 8:30-9:30 | **Opening**—crowd breakers, a brief small-group time, an encouraging message |
| | **Seminars**—Three tracks: a young-families track, a families-with-teens track, and an almost-empty-nest track |
| 9:40-10:40 | **Seminar 1** |
| 10:50-11:50 | **Seminar 2** |
| 12:00-1:00 | **Lunch** |
| 1:10-2:10 | **Seminar 3** |
| 2:20-3:20 | **Seminar 4** |
| 3:30-4:00 | **Closing for sharing and prayer** |

# PROGRAMS FOR CONNECTING STUDENTS WITH OLDER ADULTS

Like politics, family ministry makes strange bedfellows. Perhaps no combination is more unlikely—or has more potential for mutual benefit—than teenagers and senior citizens. Here are some programming ideas for connecting these two seemingly disparate age groups:

The youth programs of many churches do a good job of entertaining the young people and keeping them busy, but do little in the way of bringing them into responsible positions within the church community.
—Jack O. Balswick and Judith K. Balswick, The Family

• Once a quarter have a party or get-together at someone's house. Keep it brief, but fun.

• Perform a one-day service project together—something simple that requires teens and senior citizens to work side by side (for example, preparing Thanksgiving food packages for needy families).

• Once a month have the students spend a few hours at a different senior citizen's home, doing odd jobs or cleaning. During this time, spend a few minutes eating snacks and getting to know each other.

• Start an Adopt-a-Grandparent ministry, in which you match each student with an elderly person (or couple) in the church.

• Recruit senior citizens with specific hobbies or expertise to use their talents to help the students in the church. A retired engineer, for example, could hold half-hour math-tutoring sessions before youth group meetings.

• Assign an elderly person (or couple) to every youth ministry volunteer as a prayer support, spiritual shepherd, or supportive friend.

• Videotape senior citizens, asking them to respond to questions facing young people today. This would be a great tool for introducing or closing (if the interviewees offer guidance or advice) a lesson.

• Plan a churchwide Prom Night, asking everyone to attend dressed in the style of the year they graduated (or will graduate) from high school. (If dances don't sit well with your church, do a High School Hayride Night instead.)

# FAMILY-FRIENDLY PROGRAMS FOR JUNIOR HIGH

Are you looking to introduce a family emphasis into your junior high ministry? Try some of these programming ideas:

• Have students make a video on the topic of parent-teen conflict, in which they play the parts of both the parents and the kids.

• Sponsor a class for parents and sixth graders together about how they can deal with middle school bullies.

• On one Sunday a month conduct "Family Focus" classes, aimed at the issues kids and families face at home.

• Have students present a "This Is Your Life" program for their parents, using video and posters of old snapshots, and recruiting a few old family friends to provide some quotes. Invite the parents to a dinner party where the kids serve them dinner and put on their program.

• Host a parent-teen version of "The Newlywed Game."

• Bring in senior citizens to share some stories. Have them briefly describe what life was like for them in junior high.

• Encourage your kids to create their own parent newsletter to provide information and updates on the youth ministry.

• Sponsor a parent-teen one-day service project.

• Host a sports night for dads. (Be careful to mix the teams so that those kids whose fathers can't come will not feel left out.)

• Host a sports night for moms. (Be careful to mix the teams so that those kids whose mothers can't come will not feel left out.)

• Set up a stepparent panel to give kids an idea of what it is like to be a stepparent.

• Invite a single mom and a single dad to talk to your junior highers about the difficulty of divorce.

• In lieu of Sunday school, have your kids serve another ministry in the church—perhaps caring for toddlers, serving coffee and rolls to senior citizens, or helping the ushers count the offering money.

• Have your senior pastor surprise your group members with a visit—dressed as a biblical character.

# RITES OF PASSAGE

Most people think a rite of passage is simply a ceremony that celebrates the fact that a child is growing older. Often these rites are associated with a certain age (usually 13) or a major event (such as a high school graduation). In truth, a rite of passage is much more than a ceremony, event, or party. A rite of passage consists of two elements:

- *Rite* suggests ritual, tradition, and ceremony.

- *Passage* implies movement. In this case, it is a movement from one developmental status to another.

A ritual that involves a passage does not simply celebrate what already is. The notion of passage is symbolic of directed and proactive movement toward something which is new. A rite of passage serves a unique purpose. It is a marker of sorts—marking a change in status, responsibility, or position. It marks what *will be*, not just what *is*. The celebrant is recognized by others to be leaving one stage of maturation and entering a new one.

A rite of passage always includes three things:

- A period of preparation or training that will be necessary to the child in fulfilling the roles and responsibilities of the new status;

- A ceremony (and usually an accompanying time of celebration) that marks the change in status;

- A clear and definitive difference in how the person is treated and viewed as a result of the rite of passage.

## Make these events rites of passage in your church's family ministry

Rites of passage would seem to be a natural component of family ministry. Here are some examples of rites that may be incorporated into a family ministry:

- **Confirmation.** This is a time when a child takes responsibility for a personal faith and establishes a connection to the church.

- **Graduating from elementary-age programs to junior high programs.** This may be a class for fifth graders during the summer, but in order to qualify as a rite of passage, it must include some sort of new status, not just a change in classrooms and leadership.

- **Graduating from junior high to high school.** As with the graduation from elementary to junior high, this may be a class for eighth graders, but it also must include some significant changes in status and responsibility.

- ***Leaving home after high school.*** This may be a course for seniors, possibly with their parents, to address the transition from being an adolescent responsible to their parents to taking on adult responsibilities.

- ***Bar Mitzvah or Bas Mitzvah.*** This Jewish ceremony involves years of preparation, Hebrew school, homework, and an official change in religious status—from a child to an adult. The thirteen-year-old celebrant teaches the lesson at the ceremony and is given the responsibility for the sermon.

- ***First date.*** This may involve a time with parents (and even siblings) and possibly the church leadership, in which young people are given training in relationships, sexuality, decision making, and consequences. After this time of preparation, you could hold a community ceremony marking the kids' commitment to healthy dating patterns.

- ***Getting a driver's license.*** Typically this rite of passage is handled quietly, with little fanfare. You might consider some helpful additions to the typical preparation for this event, including seminars on decision making and automobile care, and a churchwide celebration every quarter for those kids about to

get their licenses. This doesn't have to be a major event or process, but could be a sober reminder that there are others besides kids' parents who care about how kids behave behind the wheel of a car.

• ***Becoming a missionary***. Most of the youth ministry programs that perform service and mission projects treat them like any other youth ministry event. But this is a perfect opportunity to include the church by first training and then sending out the "missionaries" as they go about their work. For adults, the axiom is "Once a missionary, always a missionary." This should also be true for those students who spend time in training, prayer, and preparation to care for and serve others in the name of Christ.

# A FAMILY COMPONENT TO CONFIRMATION MINISTRY

St. Philip the Deacon Lutheran Church in Plymouth, Minnesota, uses its confirmation program to bring church families together. Once a month during the September-to-March confirmation "season," confirmands invite their parents or guardians to the church for a meal and a program. The event is called "4-F" (faith, family, food, and fun). Each month's 4-F has a different theme—such as family communication—and generally consists of Scripture reading, activities, and a message or discussion that relate to the theme.

The leadership at St. Philip summarizes its approach this way: "Families are encouraged to view themselves as called by God to a mission as a family and to understand themselves as the primary place for faith development for family members."

# If You Want to Hurt a Family, Do This

- End your meeting 15 minutes late.
- Immediately take the kid's side in a parental conflict.
- Call the family's home after 9 p.m.
- Don't acknowledge parents or siblings when you call the family's home.
- Announce weekend camp a mere four weeks before it begins.
- Announce summer camp a mere two months before it begins.
- In your youth talks, encourage toilet-papering.

- Plan a Bible study for middle schoolers—across town, on a weekday afternoon.
- Call parents only when there is a problem with their kid.
- Imply that parents are the bad guys.
- Require or lure kids away from home three nights a week for church meetings and youth group responsibilities.
- Tell kids that homework isn't as important as youth group.
- Drive too fast.
- Speak lightly if not mockingly of the police and other authority figures.
- Do something unethical or illegal.
- Keep spotty financial records.
- Complain to one family about another family—or about your senior pastor.
- Tell students that it is healthy to separate from their parents. (See the parent handout "Individuation Not Separation" on page 117.)
- Mail information about coming events only to students (or to only one parent of a divorced home).
- Charge a fee for nearly every outing.
- Encourage youth group members to sit together during worship services.
- Tell students (or their parents) that youth camp is more important than the family vacation.
- Convince yourself that you know more about your students than their parents do.

TAKING IT HOME

# Providing Materials to Strengthen Families Where They Live

## Handouts for Parents & Teenagers

# A FAMILY-NEEDS ASSESSMENT

On the following pages is a family-needs assessment you can use as-is or adapt to your own requirements. Distribute one to each household every year or two. Spring can be a good time, for it gives you the time to collect the completed assessments, tabulate and analyze the results, then adjust your autumn programming accordingly.

The compiling and sorting of data can be done by anyone with minimal statistical experience. (Another option is to use a consultant from a local community college to compile the data.) Appoint a commission to analyze and summarize the results of the assessment. A report should first be made to the leadership of the church, including a series of ministerial and programming recommendations. The leadership should then decide on a specific course of action to address each of its concerns. The final report should be presented to the congregation, along with the specific changes and programs to be implemented as a result of the study.

# FAMILY-NEEDS ASSESSMENT

For attenders of _____
church name

Name of person completing this assessment_____Date _____

*Your candid responses enable our church to better meet the needs of each member of your family. Please answer as truthfully and accurately as you can. All answers will be kept in the strictest confidence.*

## 1. Please list all of the adults who are currently part of your household:

Name _____

☐ Male ☐ Female  Education level_____Age_____

**Occupation:**
☐ Student
☐ Military
☐ Self-employed
☐ Homemaker
☐ Homemaker and part-time income earner, self-employed
☐ Homemaker and part-time income earner, employee

☐ Skilled trade (carpenter, electrician, foreman, etc.)
☐ Skilled worker (clerical, sales, etc.)
☐ Professional
☐ Management
☐ Retired
☐ Unemployed
☐ Unemployed or retired due to disability

**Marital status:**
☐ Single, never married
☐ Single, divorced
☐ Single, widowed
☐ Separated

☐ Married to first spouse
☐ Divorced and remarried
☐ Widowed and remarried

**If married, years married to present spouse:**
☐ 2 years or less
☐ 3−6 years
☐ 7−15 years

☐ 15−29 years
☐ More than 30 years

Name _____

☐ Male ☐ Female  Education level_____Age_____

**Occupation:**
☐ Student
☐ Military
☐ Self-employed
☐ Homemaker
☐ Homemaker and part-time income earner, self-employed
☐ Homemaker and part-time income earner, employee

☐ Skilled trade (carpenter, electrician, foreman, etc.)
☐ Skilled worker (clerical, sales, etc.)
☐ Professional
☐ Management
☐ Retired
☐ Unemployed
☐ Unemployed or retired due to disability

**Marital status:**
☐ Single, never married
☐ Single, divorced
☐ Single, widowed
☐ Separated

☐ Married to first spouse
☐ Divorced and remarried
☐ Widowed and remarried

**If married, years married to present spouse:**
☐ 2 years or less
☐ 3−6 years
☐ 7−15 years

☐ 15−29 years
☐ More than 30 years

**2. How many years have you attended this church?**
- ☐ 2 years or less
- ☐ 3–5 years
- ☐ 6–10 years
- ☐ 11–20 years
- ☐ More than 20 years

**3. How often do you attend church services and activities?**
- ☐ Less than once a month
- ☐ Once a week
- ☐ Once or twice a month
- ☐ Two or more times a week

**4. Please list the names of extended families or family members living in the area (use back of this sheet if you need more room):**

Name_____ Relationship _____

Name_____ Relationship _____

Name_____ Relationship _____

Name_____ Relationship _____

**5. If you are a parent, list your children that are living at home (use back of this sheet if you need more room):**

Name_____Age____ Grade in school_____ ☐ male ☐ female

Name_____Age____ Grade in school_____ ☐ male ☐ female

Name_____Age____ Grade in school_____ ☐ male ☐ female

Name_____Age____ Grade in school_____ ☐ male ☐ female

**6. If you are a parent, check the top five areas of concern regarding your children:**
- ☐ Communication
- ☐ Alcohol and drugs
- ☐ Sexuality
- ☐ The Internet
- ☐ Expectations
- ☐ Lack of social skills
- ☐ Father's role
- ☐ College and career
- ☐ School achievement
- ☐ Friendships and peer relations
- ☐ Media—television, video games, music
- ☐ Discipline
- ☐ Telephone habits
- ☐ Relationship with Christ
- ☐ Mother's role
- ☐ Other_____
- ☐ Other_____

**7. If you are presently married, check the top five areas of concern in your marriage:**

☐ Communication     ☐ Time together
☐ Trust     ☐ Friendship
☐ Money     ☐ Future
☐ Fulfillment     ☐ Sex
☐ Spirituality     ☐ Addictions (alcohol, drugs)
☐ Pornography     ☐ Abuse
☐ Conflict resolution     ☐ Differences
☐ Career balance     ☐ Parent and in-law issues
☐ Other _____

**8. What is the best time for members of your household to be involved in a church-sponsored program? (List members next to their best times.)**

☐ Sunday mornings _____

☐ Sunday afternoons _____

☐ Sunday evenings _____

☐ Monday mornings _____

☐ Monday evenings _____

☐ Tuesday mornings _____

☐ Tuesday evenings _____

☐ Wednesday mornings _____

☐ Wednesday evenings _____

☐ Thursday mornings _____

☐ Thursday evenings _____

☐ Friday mornings _____

☐ Friday evenings _____

☐ Saturday mornings _____

☐ Saturday afternoons _____

☐ Saturday evenings _____

☐ Weekend retreats (one overnight) _____

☐ Weekend retreats (two overnights) _____

*If you need more room to answer any of the following four questions, use the back of this sheet.*

**9. About what are you satisfied with our church?**

_____
_____
_____
_____

**10. About what are you dissatisfied with our church?**

_____
_____
_____
_____

**11. How can our church help you and your family?**

_____
_____
_____
_____

**12. How can our church help you become more connected to its congregation?**

_____
_____
_____
_____

FAMILY-NEEDS ASSESSMENT—4

# A Parent Survey
# Tell Us
# What You Think

The family-needs assessment on page 99 gave you a
window into the *structure* of the families behind
your youth group or in your congregation, and some
idea of *perceived needs* within those families. This
survey, on the other hand, is particularly for parents
of teenagers in your youth group and is essentially a
chance for those adults to broadly, briefly evaluate
your youth ministry.

The first part of the survey asks for phone
numbers and addresses—indispensable for
updating your records—before asking parents for
their feelings about the influence of the church and
its youth program on their kids. So a prime time to
distribute this survey could be early summer: you
can update your records in preparation for the
following school year, as well as glean parents'
opinions about the school year that just ended
while it's still fresh in their minds.

# Parent Survey

## What do you think?

It will take you only a few minutes to complete this brief questionnaire—but to the youth ministry of this church, your responses influence a year's worth of retreats, Bible studies, service projects, and all the other aspects that make a youth ministry hum. So thanks for your time and your frank comments. Whether complimentary or critical, they'll be of great help to us.

### MOTHER

Name_____Home phone (_____)_____

Home address _____
                street                          city                  state      zip

Employer or business name_____Work phone (_____)_____

E-mail address:_____ ☐ home ☐ office

### FATHER

Name_____Home phone (_____)_____

Home address _____
(if different from above)   street                           city                  state      zip

Employer or business name_____Work phone (_____)_____

E-mail address:_____ ☐ home ☐ office

### CHILDREN

1. Child's name_____Sex___Grade___ Birthdate_____Age____

2. Child's name_____Sex___Grade___ Birthdate_____Age____

3. Child's name_____Sex___Grade___ Birthdate_____Age____

4. Child's name_____Sex___Grade___ Birthdate_____Age____

Emergency phone number (_____) _____ - _____
                                                      name

Any other important information we need to know?_____

_____

_____

# Now then, how do you feel about...

On a scale of 1 (not connected at all) to 5 (very connected), circle the number that best represents your response.

*not connected at all*                     *very connected*

1. How connected do you feel to the church?                     1  2  3  4  5

2. How connected do your children feel to the church?
*(provide a separate response for each of your children)*

_____                     1  2  3  4  5
child's name

_____                     1  2  3  4  5
child's name

_____                     1  2  3  4  5
child's name

_____                     1  2  3  4  5
child's name

3. How connected do you feel to the youth program?                     1  2  3  4  5

*not satisfied at all*                     *very satisfied*

4. How satisfied are you with the youth program?                     1  2  3  4  5

5. Briefly explain why you answered how you did on questions 1-4.

6. What are the top three things our youth ministry could do to help you in your parenting?

1.

2.

3.

7. What in your perspective is our youth ministry doing right?

8. What specific aspect(s) of our youth ministry do we need to improve?

9. Been waiting for the right time to tell the youth ministry department something? Okay, here's your chance—fire away!

# 9 FAMILY RESPONSIBILITY BUILDERS

"Before you can get your license [get ears pierced, go to the mall without adult accompaniment, go camping with friends, etc.], you've got to show more responsibility."

If you haven't said this yet, you will. For responsibility is a major issue—and source of conflict—in most American homes. Parents are constantly looking for their children to become more responsible, while kids keep looking for parents to give them more responsibility. Some of the following ideas are bound to work for you in fostering responsibility in your home:

*Success is a journey, not a destination.*

*—John Mackovic*

1 Regularly ask yourself this tough question: "If my child acts with the same amount of personal responsibility that I demonstrate, will she be okay?"

2 Whenever possible, let your child choose between two acceptable actions or activities rather than saying yes or no to just one option.

**3** When you confront a child about a wrong or poor choice, ask him to explain why he made his decision *before* you express your disagreement.

**4** Go a whole day without blaming an action or event on someone else.

**5** Walk in each other's shoes by trading chores with each other for a week.

**6** At a family meeting let all members express freely what they don't like about the household. Ask all to think of one contribution they can make toward a solution. If nothing else, each family members will at least stop complaining until a solution is worked out.

**7** Make a family "game" of counting to ten before reacting to one another.

**8** Initiate a Personal Improvement Month, during which each person in your family chooses a habit to work on replacing. Encourage each other throughout the month.

**9** At dinner discuss stories in the news or neighborhood that illustrate how people have accepted or avoided personal responsibility.

*From the newsletter* Smart Families *(Summer 1996) of Laurelglen Bible Church in Bakersfield, California*

# CAUGHT IN THE MIDDLE (OR, THE FINE ART OF STEPPARENTING)

Stepparenting is only another way of being caught in the middle. On the one side is your new spouse—the child's mother or father—and the parent in whom is vested the child's deepest feelings of security, comfort, trust, and love. On the other side is the child, perhaps bitter or insecure about the breakup of her parents' marriage. In her opinion you may be an unwelcome stranger in town.

Becoming an instant dad or mom is one of life's most difficult assignments. If you want to develop a healthy relationship with your stepchild, there are some generally accepted ground rules:

## Go slow.
Every relationship takes time. You will not become an instant hero after a vacation, a weekend, or a quality afternoon together. Be patient in displaying your emotions and affection. Wait until your new child is ready to share with you her emotions, feelings, and world.

## Make a friend.
Friendship always precedes the experience of true love. So work at becoming a pal. Talk about stuff—school, sports, the news. A shared giggle will tip you off that you are making progress.

## Keep your money in your pocket.
Material displays easily trigger a stepchild's bribery radar. Earning love with money or gifts is a sure way to impede the growth of a more genuine love that comes from the heart.

## Remember that you're not alone.
Some of us have walked in your shoes. There are answers and support to help you become the effective mom or dad your stepchild needs.

*From the newsletter* Smart Families *(Summer 1996) of Laurelglen Bible Church in Bakersfield, California*

# A SINGLE PARENT'S DEFENSE AGAINST LONELINESS

A family ministry can certainly help you raise your children alone. But a family ministry had better not ignore your own emotional issues. Like loneliness, for instance. So for starters we want to do what we can to help you make at least some of the following suggestions into joyful habits.

• Accept what can't be changed.

• Refuse to retreat into a shell.

• Be realistic about just how green the grass really is on the other side.

• Cultivate a spirit of thankfulness.

• Refuse to see yourself as merely treading water.

• Reach out to others.

• Maintain your physical health.

• Establish well-defined goals for yourself.

• Rejuvenate your spiritual sensitivity.

*From the newsletter* Smart Families *(Summer 1996) of Laurelglen Bible Church in Bakersfield, California*

# YOU, TOO, CAN REDUCE CONFLICT OVER CHORES!

How many of the parent-teen conflicts in your home are somehow related to chores? If you're a parent, you are (or soon will be) a veteran of chore wars. Still, there *are* ways to reduce the friction and stress that usually follow the assignment of household chores.

• Teach *skills*, not chores. In order to do this, you'll need to make materials accessible to your kids. You'll also need to demonstrate the task for them. Work alongside them the first few times they attempt the chore. As you teach move from the simple to the difficult. In your effort to teach your children, make sure that you never redo their work.

• Keep in mind that kids remember 10 percent of what they hear, 50 percent of what they see, and 90 percent of what they do.

• Use regular family meeting times to set goals and standards and to assign tasks. You'll also need to set aside time to discuss, celebrate, and reward everyone's progress.

• Post charts showing assigned tasks and deadlines.

• Remember that kids tend to rebel when they are given only unpleasant jobs or when extra requirements are added after a task is first explained.

• Ask yourself this question: What am I doing for my children that, if left undone, would teach them to care for that particular part of their own world?

• Be willing to let your children suffer natural and logical consequences for their actions.

• Step in and help your child finish a task rather than reward incomplete work.

• Don't set a training goal or consequence that you are not prepared to follow through on.

• Remember that as you teach kids their responsibilities, your goal is to work yourself out of a job.

*From the newsletter* Smart Families, *Summer 1996, of Laurelglen Bible Church in Bakersfield, California.*

# 15 CREATIVE WAYS TO TELL YOUR KIDS "I LOVE YOU!"

How can you creatively let your kids know that you love them? Here are some ideas to get you started.

1 Take them on a date once a month—and let them choose the activity.

2 Take out an ad in your local newspaper to publicize their latest accomplishments.

3 Write something encouraging on a Post-It note and stick it on their homework or on their napkin in their lunch bag.

4 Write them a poem and read it to them at bedtime.

5 Kidnap them unexpectedly for a walk or a meal.

6 For no special reason, throw a surprise party and invite their best friends.

7 Plan a family slumber party, complete with popcorn, videos, a fire, and late-night tales.

Some parents find it difficult to verbalize their love for their children. Strangely, the existence of love cannot be assumed. If it is unspoken, it may be doubted. Parents need to tell their children they love them.
—Merton Strommen and Irene Strommen, The Five Cries of Parents

**8** Take them breakfast in bed (whether pancakes from your kitchen or a McScramble from down the street).

**9** Plan a progressive date for them and a few friends—you know, Burger King for appetizers, a park for the first course, a driving range for the main course, and then finish off the evening with a drive-in movie in someone's garage.

**10** Arrange for someone with celebrity status in your children's eyes to phone them.

**11** Make an acrostic of your child's name, with each letter beginning a word or phrase that describes a character trait you admire.

**12** Give them a framed picture of yourself— framed and signed, "With love..."

**13** When they're asleep, give them light kisses until they wake up; then quickly put the family dog next to their face.

**14** Decorate their room while they are away.

**15** Treat your daughter to a makeover or your son to a half-hour massage.

# "THINGS I WISH MY DAD KNEW"

Members of a high school group in Texas were asked, "What do you wish your dad knew?" These are some of their responses:

• *I do look up to you, Dad!*

• *I don't thank you as much as I should.*

• *That I'm alive.*

• *That my sister isn't perfect, either.*

• *That I love him and want him to be closer to me.*

• *I truly respect, admire, and appreciate you.*

• *Daddy, calm down and relax. These years will soon be over and we will both see that we have grown and learned.*

> Simply put, even the best mothers cannot be good fathers.
> —*Barbara D. Whitehead, "Women and the Future of Fatherhood,"* Women's Quarterly

• *I really do have talents.*

• *I forgive you.*

• *I know he tries real hard, and I respect him for that.*

• *My shoe size*

• *How hard I work to do my best for him, even though it is never good enough*

- *I love him.*

- *I need the love of more than one parent*

- *That I want a relationship with him, but I don't want rejection*

- *My best is good enough.*

- *That even though he has no idea what he's doing . . . I still love him A LOT! Thanks for trying your best.*

- *I am not and never will be a famous tennis, basketball, or baseball player, but I am good at what I do.*

- *I believe everything he tells me and trust him....know he's right and I care.*

- *I love you, man!*

# INDIVIDUATION, NOT SEPARATION

Most teenagers have a burning desire to separate themselves from their parents, right? Well, maybe not. Consider the following definitions:

• *Separate* means to move away from, to disconnect.

• *Individuate* means to find one's own identity and sense of personal autonomy within the context of family attachment.

It is a popular, widespread myth that adolescents desire and need to *separate* from their families. In truth the adolescent journey is marked by a process called *individuation,* in which kids discover (1) who they are, and (2) that their choices matter. Individuation is most easily and rewardingly accomplished when there is a strong sense of attachment to both parents—especially the father—during this time of transition. This attachment is marked by a perception of trust, good communication, and an overall sense of closeness.

Youth workers would do well to help their students recognize their inborn desire to be connected with their parents and family, and to help parents understand that the period of individuation is not a time to let go relationally, but a time to lovingly protect and guide their kids while encouraging a deeper sense of independent living.

Is it really all that important to spend time with your kids? Social scientists John DeFrain and Nick Stinnett asked 1,500 school kids, "What do you think makes a family happy?" Their most frequent answer: doing things together.
—*Mike Yorkey, "A Time Well Spent,"* New Man

# CHRISTMAS IDEAS FOR FAMILY MINISTRY

Perhaps no other time of year brings families together like Christmas. Take advantage of the unique family bonding opportunities the season offers by trying out one or more of the following ideas.

Read Isaiah 9:6–7 and 40:3–5 together. Draw and cut out self-portraits as a family and hang them on your Christmas tree. Write on the back of each picture a favorite Bible verse or spiritual quote of that person.

Read one verse each night from Luke's Christmas story (Luke 2:1–20) during the month of December. Ask each person in the family to make one comment about the verse before anyone says anything else. Once everyone is finished, discuss for a few minutes the thought that sparked the most interest, controversy, or laughter.

Secretly have each person in the family make an ornament for every other person in the family. When you trim the tree, save these ornaments for last. As family members bring out their ornaments one by one to place on the tree, have them share what each person means to them.

Commit to having an Advent ceremony at least once a week with another family (or two) from the church. You might even consider having a churchwide ceremony every week after church over brunch.

# GOD THE PARENT: THE MODEL OF BIBLICAL PARENTING

God himself is the ultimate parent, says Myron Chartier in "Parenting: A Theological Model" (*Journal of Psychology and Theology*, 1978). Chartier points out that God reveals his parental love in at least seven different ways:

**1** God cares for his children (Luke 15:11–32; I Peter 5:7).

**2** God is responsive to his children's needs (Genesis 9:8–17, John 3:16, Titus 3:3–7).

**3** God bestows the richest of gifts on his children, including his Son and his Holy Spirit as Comforter (Psalm 84:11, Psalm 112:9, Matthew 7:11, John 3:16, 1 Timothy 6:17, Hebrews 2:4).

**4** God values, cherishes, and shows his respect for his children (Isaiah 33:6, Luke 14:10–11, 2 Corinthians 4:13–15).

**5** God knows his children, for Jesus entered our world as a human being (John 1:14, Philippians 2:5–8, Hebrews 2:17–18, 4:15). This knowledge touches us to the core (Psalm 44:21, John 2:25).

**6** God forgives his children (Matthew 26:28, John 3:16–17, Ephesians 1:7).

**7** God disciplines his children for their own good (Proverbs 3:11–12, Hebrews 12:5–8, Revelation 3:19).

# 15 Creative Ways to Tell Your Parents "I Love You!"

You know that actions speak louder than words—so take some action to let your parents know you love them!

**1** Invite them out to breakfast and pay for their meals.

**2** Put together a video collage featuring them.

**3** Wash their car without telling them.

**4** Give them one of your paychecks.

**5** Surprise them at work with a card and a flower.

**6** Throw a surprise dinner party and invite their best friends.

**7** Stay off the phone for one week.

**8** Stay home evenings for a week and do what they want to do.

**9** Toilet paper their room, and then clean it up the next morning.

**10** Make them breakfast in bed.

**11** Give them 15-minute foot massages.

**12** Call them at work just to say hi and chat a bit.

**13** Do the laundry for a week.

**14** Sit with them in church for a month.

**15** Write them a note with "I love you"—and 15 reasons why.

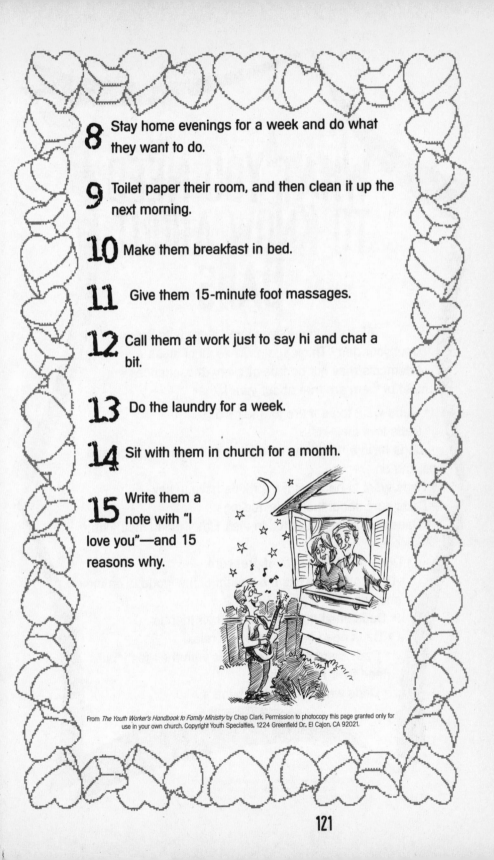

# WHAT YOU NEED TO KNOW ABOUT DADS

Think you know everything there is to know about your dad? Think again. While all of these statements may not be true of every dad, chances are most of them are true about *your* father.

- Dads want to be there for their kids.
- Dads love their kids.
- Dads have a hard time balancing between letting go and holding on.
- Dads want to hear what their kids have to say.
- Dads care about their kids' feelings.
- Dads are more interested in their kids than in their kids' success.
- Dads are under a lot of pressure.
- Dads often feel like the weight of the world is on their shoulders.
- Dads need their kids to be their friends.
- Dads need time to rest and relax.
- Dads want to help their kids with their faith, but need their kids' help.
- Dads want to be good fathers.

# WHAT YOU NEED TO KNOW ABOUT MOMS

Think your mom is pretty predictable? Think again. While all of these statements may not be true of every mom, chances are most of them are true about your mother.

• Moms are more than waitresses, house cleaners, and chauffeurs.

• Moms need someone to listen to how *their* day went.

• Moms want to be involved in their kids' lives.

• Moms' smiles sometimes cover hurt or sadness.

• Moms can tell when something is wrong and a good

talk is needed.

• Moms will always be there, no matter how bad things get.

• Moms hate it when kids try to come between them and their husbands.

• Moms have a hard time letting themselves be sick.

• Moms need a life, too.

• Moms love it when you remember details like this:

A Gallup survey (February, 1990) [found that] men were identified by 74 percent of the respondents as the most likely spouse to handle minor home repairs, and by 63 percent as the spouse most likely to do yard work. Women, on the other hand, were more likely to do all or most of the laundry (79 percent), care for the children when they are sick (72 percent), clean the house (69 percent), wash the dishes (68 percent) and pay the bills (65 percent). They were viewed as the spouse more likely to be the primary discipliner of the children...On balance, it does appear that the typical mother is likely to endure a more-than-equal share of the parenting load.

—*George Barna,* The Future of the American Family

# WHAT YOU NEED TO KNOW ABOUT PARENTS...AND ABOUT STEPPARENTS

You may be surprised to learn that you don't know everything there is to know about your parents. While all of these statements may not be true of every mom and dad, chances are most of them are true of your parents.

☑ Parents are often tired.

☑ Parents are scared of the future.

☑ Parents love their kids.

☑ Parents are nervous about the world.

☑ Parents are stressed.

☑ Parents wish they had more fun.

☑ Parents are often lonely.

☑ Parents do not always "have it all together," regardless of how they seem.

☑ Parents want to be taken seriously.

☑ Parents, on the inside, often still think of themselves as being in high school.

**How hard have you tried to get to know your stepparent?** You may be surprised at what you learn. While all of these statements may not be true of every stepparent, chances are most of them are true of yours.

☑ Stepparents are trying as hard as they can.

☑ Stepparents often don't know what to do.

☑ Stepparents would like to be friends with their stepchildren.

☑ Stepparents don't want to be the bad guys.

☑ Stepparents don't want to steal your birth parent from you.

☑ Stepparents don't want to take the place of your absent parent.

☑ Stepparents need your acceptance.

☑ Stepparents love their spouse, and want to love you.

☑ Stepparents need your help to know what to do and what not to do.

☑ Stepparents have a very, very hard job.

The author is available for speaking and
consulting on family-ministry issues.
You may contact him at 818-584-5608,
or by e-mail at cclark@fuller.edu.

# Youth Specialties Titles

## Professional Resources

Administration, Publicity, & Fundraising (Ideas Library)
Developing Student Leaders
Equipped to Serve: Volunteer Youth Worker Training Course
Help! I'm a Junior High Youth Worker!
Help! I'm a Sunday School Teacher!
Help! I'm a Volunteer Youth Worker!
How to Expand Your Youth Ministry
How to Speak to Youth...and Keep Them Awake at the Same Time
One Kid at a Time: Reaching Youth through Mentoring
A Youth Ministry Crash Course
The Youth Worker's Handbook to Family Ministry

## Youth Ministry Programming

Camps, Retreats, Missions, & Service Ideas (Ideas Library)
Compassionate Kids: Practical Ways to Involve Your Students in Mission and Service
Creative Bible Lessons in John: Encounters with Jesus
Creative Bible Lessons in Romans: Faith on Fire!
Creative Bible Lessons on the Life of Christ
Creative Junior High Programs from A to Z, Vol. 1 (A-M)
Creative Meetings, Bible Lessons, & Worship Ideas (Ideas Library)
Crowd Breakers & Mixers (Ideas Library)
Drama, Skits, & Sketches (Ideas Library)
Dramatic Pauses
Facing Your Future: Graduating Youth Group with a Faith That Lasts
Games (Ideas Library)
Games 2 (Ideas Library)
Great Fundraising Ideas for Youth Groups
More Great Fundraising Ideas for Youth Groups
Great Retreats for Youth Groups
Greatest Skits on Earth
Greatest Skits on Earth, Vol. 2
Holiday Ideas (Ideas Library)
Hot Illustrations for Youth Talks
More Hot Illustrations for Youth Talks
Incredible Questionnaires for Youth Ministry
Junior High Game Nights
Kickstarters: 101 Ingenious Intros to Just about Any Bible Lesson
Memory Makers
More Junior High Game Nights
Play It! Great Games for Groups

Play It Again! More Great Games for Groups
Special Events (Ideas Library)
Spontaneous Melodramas
Super Sketches for Youth Ministry
Teaching the Bible Creatively
Up Close and Personal: How to Build Community in Your Youth Group
Wild Truth Bible Lessons
Worship Services for Youth Groups

## Discussion Starter Resources

Discussion & Lesson Starters (Ideas Library)
Discussion & Lesson Starters 2 (Ideas Library)
4th-6th Grade TalkSheets
Get 'Em Talking
High School TalkSheets
High School TalkSheets: Psalms and Proverbs
Junior High TalkSheets
Junior High TalkSheets: Psalms and Proverbs
Keep 'Em Talking! Real-Life Dilemmas That Teach
More High School TalkSheets
More Junior High TalkSheets
What If...? 450 Thought-Provoking Questions to Get Teenagers Talking, Laughing, and Thinking
Would You Rather...? 465 Provocative Questions to Get Teenagers Talking

## Clip Art

ArtSource Vol. 1—Fantastic Activities
ArtSource Vol. 2—Borders, Symbols, Holidays, and Attention Getters
ArtSource Vol. 3—Sports
ArtSource Vol. 4—Phrases and Verses
ArtSource Vol. 5—Amazing Oddities and Appalling Images
ArtSource Vol. 6—Spiritual Topics
ArtSource Vol. 7—Variety Pack
ArtSource Vol. 8—Stark Raving Clip Art
ArtSource CD-ROM (contains Vols. 1–7)

## Videos

EdgeTV
The Heart of Youth Ministry: A Morning with Mike Yaconelli
Next Time I Fall in Love Video Curriculum
Understanding Your Teenager Video Curriculum

## Student Books

Grow For It Journal
Grow For It Journal through the Scriptures
Wild Truth Journal for Junior Highers